Boecher

MW01155159

Ireland

Helen Arnold

RSVP

RAINTREE
STECK-VAUGHN
PUBLISHERS
The Steck-Vaughn Company

Austin, Texas

Published by Raintree Steck-Vaughn Publishers, an imprint of Steck-Vaughn Company

A ZOË BOOK

Editors: Kath Davies, Pam Wells
Design: Sterling Associates
Map: Julian Baker
Production: Grahame Griffiths

Library of Congress Cataloging-in-Publication Data

Arnold, Helen.
    Ireland / Helen Arnold.
        p. cm. — (Postcards from)
    "A Zoë Book" — T.p.verso
    Includes index.
    Summary: A collection of fictional postcards, written as if by young people visiting Ireland, describes various sights and life in the Emerald Isle.
    ISBN 0-8172-4026-8 (hardcover). — ISBN 0-8172-6217-2 (softcover)
    1. Ireland—Description and travel—Juvenile literature.
    [1. Ireland—Description and travel. 2. Postcards.] I. Title. II. Series.
    DA978.2.A76 1997
    914.1504'824—dc20   95–52927
                                                                      CIP
                                                                       AC

Printed and bound in the United States

2   3   4   5   6   7   8   9   0   WZ   04   03   02   01

Photographic acknowledgments

The publishers wish to acknowledge, with thanks, the following photographic sources:

Adam Woolfitt - cover bl; / Michael Short 8; / Teresa Black 12; / Charles Bowman 22; / Robert Harding Picture Library; Impact Photos / Paul O'Driscoll - cover tl, 24; / Geray Sweeney 10, 18, 20; / S. Shepheard 28; Zefa - cover r, title page, 6, 14, 16, 26.

The publishers have made every effort to trace the copyright holders, but if they have inadvertently overlooked any, they will be pleased to make the necessary arrangement at the first opportunity.

Contents

All the words that appear in **bold** are explained in the Glossary on page 30.

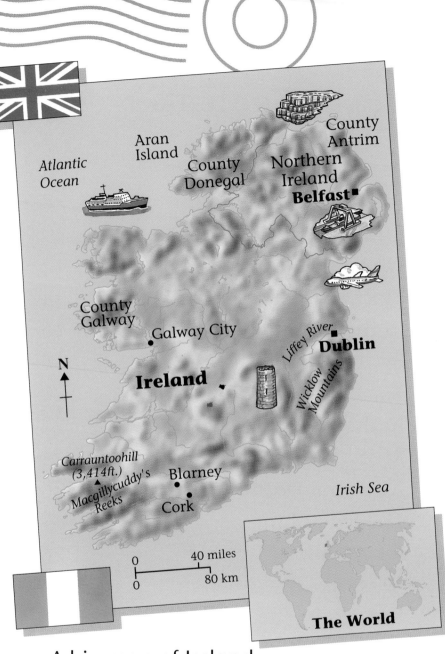

Atlantic
Ocean

Aran
Island

County
Donegal

County
Antrim

Northern
Ireland

Belfast■

County
Galway

Galway City

Liffey River■ **Dublin**

Ireland .

Wicklow
Mountains

N

Carrauntoohill
(3,414ft.)
▲
Macgillycuddy's
Reeks

Blarney
.
.
Cork

Irish Sea

0   40 miles
├───┤
0   80 km

The World

A big map of Ireland
and a small map of the world

Dear Linda,

You can see Ireland in red on the small map. The plane took over eight hours to fly here from Chicago. We flew across the United States and then over the Atlantic Ocean.

Love,

Bill

P.S. Mom says that it rains a lot on this **island**, so all the fields look fresh and green. There are some very wet fields here that are called bogs.

A busy street in the middle of Dublin

Dear Shane,

Dublin is the **capital** city of the **Republic** of Ireland. *Eire* is the Irish name for this part of the island. About two million people live here. Most people speak English. Some speak the Irish language called *Gaelic*.

Your friend,

Brad

P.S. Dublin is on the east coast of Ireland. The Liffey River flows through the city.

A food market in Dublin

Dear Ben,

We went to this market today. The food in our little hotel is great. They make special bread for us and potato cakes. For breakfast we have bacon and eggs with sausages.

Your friend,

Keith

P.S. My uncle says that long ago potatoes were the main food for most people in Ireland. Sometimes the potato **crop** did not grow. When this happened, many people died from hunger.

The church and the Round Tower, Glendalough

Dear Jan,

Glendalough is in the Wicklow Mountains. We came here by coach from Dublin. We climbed to the top of the mountains. We could see a lovely lake in the valley below us.

Your friend,

Kevin

P.S. Grandad took us to see the church and the Round Tower. The tower was built by a **saint** called Kevin. He lived more than a thousand years ago.

A small boat arriving at Inishbofin Island, County Galway

Dear Pippa,

We have not seen many cars in the countryside. People here like to use the buses and the trains. I like to ride on the buses. Dad uses Irish money called *punts* to pay the fare.

Love,

Alex

P.S. Dad says that there are lots of small islands around the Irish coast. Some people travel on boats called **ferries** to get to them.

Blarney Castle in County Cork

Dear Meg,

The castle is in the village called Blarney. **Tourists** come here to kiss the Blarney Stone. There is a story, or **legend**, that if you kiss the stone, people will love to hear you talk.

Love,

Charles

P.S. Mom did not come to Blarney. She went shopping in Cork. Cork is the second biggest city in the Republic of Ireland. It has rained a lot here, but it is not cold.

An old cottage in County Galway

Dear Fran,

We are staying in a country cottage like this one. It is in Galway on the west coast of Ireland. Galway faces out toward the United States. The Atlantic Ocean is in between.

Love,

Rachel

P.S. Our cottage is next door to a farm. Every Saturday the farmers go to Galway City. They have food stands in the market. Mr. and Mrs. Rooney sell cheese there.

Fishing boats and Aran Island,
County Donegal

Dear Martin,

We have reached the north of Ireland. We are staying in a fishing village in Donegal. Today we went for a walk along the beach. We saw some islands nearby.

Your friend,

Tim

P.S. My uncle took us for a walk to the top of a high cliff called Slieve League. It was very scary. There was a steep drop to the ocean on one side and high cliffs on the other.

The Giant's Causeway, County Antrim

Dear Mia,

These strange stones are called the Giant's **Causeway**. People come from around the world to see the stones. Thousands of years ago, a **volcano** made the stones this shape.

Love,

Rob

P.S. My sister says that there is a story about the stones. Long ago, a giant threw them into the sea. Then the giant used them as stepping stones when he fought a Scottish giant.

In the middle of Belfast

Dear Lucy,

Belfast is the capital city of Northern Ireland. The streets are full of people and noisy **traffic**. There is a place for building ships here and a place for making cars.

Your friend,

Amanda

P.S. My aunt says that she studied at the **university** here. It is called Queen's University. There is a lovely, big park near the university. Belfast has lots of parks.

A fast game of hurling between teams
from Tipperary and Clare

Dear Derek,

Have you heard of hurling or Gaelic football? Hurling is very fast. It is something like field hockey. In Gaelic football you can punch and carry the ball. You can kick it, too.

Love,

Ted

P.S. My dad says you have to be good to play golf in Ireland. Some Irish golf players are world famous. Racehorses that are born and trained in Ireland are sent all over the world.

Christmas Day is the special day that
children in Ireland like best.

Dear Stella,

There are special days for all kinds of things here. People dress up in their best clothes to go to church. Sometimes people sing and dance in the streets at **festivals**.

Love,

Alma

P.S. St. Patrick is the **patron** saint of Ireland. March 17 is St. Patrick's Day. Everyone here has a holiday on that day.

A young boy waving the flag of the
Republic of Ireland

Dear Laura,

This is the flag for the Republic of Ireland. The Irish people there choose their own leaders. The head of this country is called the president.

Love,

Justin

P.S. Dad says that Northern Ireland is part of the United Kingdom. The other countries are England, Scotland, and Wales. The United Kingdom is ruled from London in England.

Glossary

Capital: The town or city where people who rule the country meet. It is not always the biggest city in the country.

Causeway: A path that is higher than the water around it

Crops: Plants that farmers grow, such as potatoes

Ferry: A boat that carries people across the water

Island: A piece of land that has water all around it

Legend: An old story that many people believe, even though it may not be quite true

Patron: Somebody who looks after a person or a thing

P.S.: This stands for Post Script. A postscript is the part of a card or letter that is added at the end, after the person has signed it.

Republic: A country where the people choose their leaders. There is no king or queen.

Saint: A holy person

Tourists: People who are on a vacation away from home

Traffic: The cars, trucks, and bikes that carry people or goods from place to place

University: A place where students go to study, after they have left school

Volcano: A mountain that throws out molten or melted rock and hot ash

Index